APPLIED FREEDOM

APPLIED FREEDOM

selected poems

NIKOLAY BOYCHEV

Library and Archives Canada
The Canadian ISBN Service System (CISS)

Boychev, Nikolay, 1989 -
Applied Freedom : selected poems / Nikolay Boychev
ISBN 978-0-9936748-0-8

To my parents, Mariela and Karol

"In determination of prevention,
as a form of aid to human development,
I will attempt to comprehend meaning."

FROM THE POEM *Sketch*

APPLIED FREEDOM

CONTENTS

FOREWORD

By Jessica Riehm

Inspiring and contemporary, a man of passion, are words I would use to best describe Nikolay Boychev. Nikolay displays so much of raw emotion in his poetry or any work of art. He perfectly identifies with what it means to be human, lost, devastated, aroused, and flamboyant in a manner that questions if one truly understands these concepts.

As a result of his inferno of passion being subdued by his logical disposition, Nikolay is the ideal poet. His clever and often complex juxtapositions offer a new take on ideals such as family, relationships, independence, and interdependence. The book reminds the reader that life can be as simple as it is complicated, all while forcing one to question their own inner demons in light of the truths that emerge in the pieces.

The climatic stanzas and works of this book, as well as my awe and enthusiasm for the development of the truly talented author that is Nikolay Boychev, forces me to write this foreword. A work so utterly invigorating such as this book demands special recognition.

JESSICA RIEHM
Student-at-Law
Toronto, Ontario

Bushes Grow

irony

He wears a patched cape and carries a walking-stick,
as if there is no energy, or need to dress.
He never sees beauty,
indifferent to others, thinks of them as simpletons,
and categorizes attachments as meaningless snippets.

She is charming,
but her presence is repetitive and warred down,
which describes the patched caped man perfectly.
All of her features appeal to him,
but he only notices later.

symbolism

He is a grim crane without a flock,
acting like a nomad.
His name is most impassionate and lacks fire.
At the moment of departure between them,
he will be granted a chance to have a life experience.

Human and nature converge on the trail.
Life is born as bushes grow.
There is less order to allow free thinking
and with the haze being clear,
he can now see his own reflection.

climax

Thought-provoking fights awaken a duel
with his regular pulse-lacking state of existence.
He is no longer static, trapped,
because there are refreshing, lively notions.
But with the track disappearing, so is his chance to live.

Their paths cross,
because they want to experience each other's life,
but only she understands the necessity.
He has become a half-man,
never being exposed to another's needs.

Character & Conscience

This arrogance…
the reluctant compassion for another
in the essence of struggle,
effaces vividness in life.

Such instances,
conformable indications,
exceeding executions,
archive new monumental tensions.

These are the two to twelve second durations
retaining the greater impact
of the issues at hand,
interchanging the stressful views towards others.

This mistrust…
the reverence begged to emerge alive
within the realization of togetherness,
insults the vitality of living for character.

Squatting, then scampering with disregard,
sliding over the sides.
ALL of it manifests, as the true way to feel a human presence,
foreshadowing another's life in between.

This dignity…
as if destined, is the only chance for survival,
breathing, sweating in the midst of differentiation,
acquaints a relieving unison with others' souls.

Choices to Live By

Commitment is a colossal factor in achieving a dream.
Choices blindfold by the extreme influence of self-esteem.
Presence of others builds up the pressure in your mind.
Fear of reality, and self-sacrificing make you feel confined.

Nourished by your talents, you continue to fight.

Discipline is an idea capable of making you stronger.
Proficiency is being improved by competing longer.
Brilliancy, failure can have the same meaning at a time.
Being ambitious, but not trusting is the true crime.

Cherishing your gifts fulfills your life as a true winner.

Society's hardships are the greatest test of all.
If your dreams are of significant importance, you will always stand tall.
Pretending is only good enough to say nice try.
Proving of having a bright soul is the only way to never say goodbye.

Deliberating your actions will guide you on the right path…

Clarity Within

Can I retain clarity through metaphors?
Can I decode meaning in simulacrums of common objects?
The materials are there, but my *strive* may be lost in the ambiguous.

How can I ensure communal development?
Artistry needs not be invited to a personal experience,
but my morals must first be comprehended.

Can I find the voice of the central message?
Am I acquiring the state of the lived, wrapped across neutrality?
Visualizing my own poverty, for it will provide an awakening.

How long will I endure within repetition?
When will I highlight the righteous words?
The links must be discovered, the strands and binaries included in the details.

What are the comparative applications?
Where was the beginning of the contrasting end?
My mindset must be uncovered among the broken glass.

Dripping, drying, I need to fix the initial mirror on time,
rediscover gaining, forgetting,
and allow the constancy of interpretation.

That is the entity,
which can never be manipulated,
or taken away.

Crying Tears

A timeless daydream…
The sky's canvas is brilliant among an epiphany of clouds.
The heart's soul is pace-less, though provoked, impatient.

People's sins are the cornerstone of reality…
A child is the unwilling purity in nature.
A woman's beauty neglects circular superficialities.

Feelings are tormented,
Emotions are scattered
Into the surroundings.

Vision diminishes in thick fogs…
Emptiness is found in misty backgrounds.
Completeness is lost on a mountain of crystals.

Collectively…
Heavenly tears liberate identities.
Dust particles of rusty sensations drop in puddles endlessly.

Fragile hopes of love repent relentlessly…
A universe's sunrays glimpse through the rancid air.
An ocean's waves rush down states of delirium.

Notions of truthfulness begin to coruscate…
The ruins helplessly become nostalgic.
Gentle hands rejuvenate the lenses.

Insides of tomorrow are revealing today.
The curtains open
AND
Smiles are born again.

Emergence

A script of its own title.
A directed collision with awkward affections.
A written production with people all too distinct.

The opening scene is set at an angle.
The thematic significance of interactions is the way individuals feel real.
Now, they can share their natural instincts without hesitation.

The shot duration is fixed.
There are no limitations of expression, or measured consequences,
But a sincere overlap of personal experiences.

The collision is governing the course of mentality.
Vantage points showcase unique personal traits-he laughs, while she cries.
Inevitable judgements are applied through prejudicial thoughts and prejudicial actions.

The lighting is adjusted.
Terms and expressions are symbolically cultivated,
Where a catastrophe links them all again.

Despite previous acts of humility,
The behavior, and long-term effects of interpersonal connections emerge,
Yet again.

Equilibrium Position

Proof of evidence,
no shortage of food in a complex world.
The sound is lost,
imitated by wanting forgiveness.

We preserved awareness through value,
an attempt to life.
We understood the feelings, but forgot the language,
the slowing of lacking roots.

Refusal of birth,
common anger.
The ritual stands as a border
on which familiarity counteracts possibility.
Irony of ruin,
equilibrium is shifted.
Gentleness brings pain.

The previous view
turns out to be misleading.
Shame, grief,
the acting products of sustainability.
Smooth poles between the hands,
we are no longer children.

Spectators of human imperfections
altered unconditional love,
overcoming natural goodness,
and bringing upon betrayal.

Within each moment, we stand together,
accepting a portion of guilt.
The escaped fear from childhood has returned
to discover the impossible correlation.

The two always mix,
as removing one from the other
and living in this pattern
is untrue.

Familiar Echoes

Eight actors sit inside, what once was a gracious hall,
now a centenarian, burdened theatre.
On its unusable stage, texture slowly decaying,
each is about to perform the same contrasts of two people within one.

The acts will be depicted with limited props,
but fully utilizing the hall's space.
This progression, accompanied by familiar echoes,
dazzles with vivid oppression, frustration, and disappointment.

The actors perform within a rehearsal,
without costumes, or special effects.
It is real, appealing, but colorless and inexpensive,
as in the actual production.

The repertoire is nearly identical, capturing the same self-torture,
missing passion, and feeding on endless bitterness.
Throughout, there is a more obvious expression of laughter.
A recurring discrepancy in every act is the kissing and hugging at departures.

Two of the characters are intimate,
not fitting with the rest, disrupting everyone's daily routines.
After they leave, all habits are returned,
and liberation is possible.

There is no action, hysterical drama,
but the actors are interlinked by the unpleasantness of their close proximity.
There is no familial connection, clues to individual behavior,
except in reclusiveness, or during an irritable conversation.

There is the perpetual sense of being frozen in time,
the correlation between mood and weather changes.
There is still no tragedy, only the rearranged,
functionally preserved comedic feeling.

The most noted difference is the ending,
cutting many lines,
but having the same message,
-"we shall be at rest".

Flying the Wall

bonded relationship,
overturned-existence.
engaging emotions,
closed thoughts, traits tilting sideways.

demonstrates

understands

He

assures

emphasizes

in the moment,
exchanging the hardship,
shooting down at Themselves,
screaming out of mental and physical disturbances.

Me
not You
Somebody else
not You

resembling the composure in seeing an opportunity,
They exhibit a form of self-esteem,
reaching across the lap, almost squished together,
gaining the power to confide again.

forgets

realizes

She

perseveres

preserves

missing belts and blades,
flying away from impotency.
there is a moment of panic,
but It is freely substituted.

Hysteria Image

a clock screamed.

                sleeping on an unfamiliar bed-side,

                              unsure of the alarm's resurgence,

                                my eyes hardly opened.

                loud in the darkness,

I turned it off and
lifted myself-up.
the walls protruding,
the ceiling minimized,

                light-impenetrable windows and

                    their waving curtains

painted overtaking shadows.

surroundings like never before.
my painful spine,
aching knuckles

                slipped all memories.

                                bewildered,

                            I walked through a corridor

                with missing appeal.

an isolating house,
strange portraits,

              and shelves with decorative casings.

enigmatic neural streams,
improbable comprehension.
I headed for a face-wash,
looked into a mirror.

                cold sweat crawled down,

                            brief detail toyed my perception.

                          colorful features suddenly exquisite

                  -deep blues and

glistening yellows,
unexpectedly long and
fuzzy hairs,
patterned eyebrows and

                      ears.

                in desperate search,

                          I anxiously stretched in all directions.

                attaining a full body image,

evident torments
and faulty resemblances.

I remember

Seaming idealism,
actions allowed majestic results.
Promised serenity.
The uncultivated were convinced of removed opacities,
of life's carriage with confirmed cleanliness.

Immigrated wretchedness.
Confrontations of our new origin,
and lack of balancing the cultural warmth.
The words now senseless in their context,
as semblance walks proudly.

Where is the chance to live?
Naivety clouds our inner struggles.
Can't see,
can't choose.
Limited resources, conditions.
We should have kept time and matched every step.

Does it resemble positivity?
Heavy smells, dense weight,
yellow grease.
Escape is outside.

Where are the ceilings, the transition of platforms, and identifiable surfaces?
Jostling for space,
not supposed to confess.
I remember that I loved.

Letter from the Past

In a skeptical, but realistic debate over eternal policy,
She efficiently relates to the amicable.
Opening and concluding with unresolved separations,
undeniably incisive, proficient,
She only mentions positivistic historical attributes via corrupted appeals.

Her chaotic emotions substitute reasoning.
Her amiable ethics make hope vulnerable,
as our greatest obstacles miss bearing by the harsh,
simplistic generalizations.
Her logic is the most insidious,
enforcing disarray, untrustworthiness.

She is convincing,
touching upon beauty and embarrassment,
the main contraries an individual would sense.
She is respectful, offering proudness,
but her neighbourly status is an accusing force.
She is delicate,
there is no reason to think differently.
She can replace concern with a told legend,
and criticize with silly optimism.

The letter addresses ambassadors of transitioning.
Empty, but full of controversy,
cleverly written with transparent arguments,
it threatens, and raises more questions than answers.
Her work is evidently a tampering attitude,
wording all our downfalls.

Love Perhaps

Merging social disparities,
and portrayals of the rural against the urban,
rhythms lived to the fullest may be conveyed, and others,
like a pendulum by offered contradictions with uncertain resolutions.

I am a superfluous man,
but my self-realization is sparked by her.
She unravels the truest insights of my youth,
perhaps, giving me purpose.

I should have a family,
perhaps, considered as all duty-oriented at times.
I should have midlife crisis,
perhaps, considered as all conscience at times.

I am an antediluvian man,
but cannot encompass the most essential daily aspect.
I can analyze and critique philosophy, verse,
but cannot cope with her expression, pain.

While walking along in the present,
on opposite ends stand the predictable past and future.
Both are hardly separable,
since I see everything as vanishing into memories.

I am afraid to live,
but at her core, hidden,
is my attempt to understand the soul,
which provides a sense of direction.

Perhaps, I am old from the beginning,
until there is an interruption.
Making me feel youthful, perhaps,
such instances last minutes of enlightenment.

Lullaby

I am a white horse,
manifesting thoughts of solitude.
This ability is enforced,
as my days are restricted to an obscure enclosure.

Bought and sold,
I am kept as fruit, discarded as waste.
My companions, own love, and future,
all traded away.

I am a stained virgin,
always craving a new place.
I enslave my horizons for entertainment,
only cherishing their materialistic transformations.

Neither I,
nor animals
opt to be detached,
as each feeling fits together, and encourages the next.

I am a classical composer,
having a unique lullaby every time.
The tone varies with the magnitude of changes and deceit,
determining my conquest for simplicity.

The disinclined isolation within
fuels my desire for belonging.
I will go to the moon on my path to salvation,
to find a more profound meaning in life.

I am a relic.
Despite the vast space,
it is inherent in my nature to fall victim.
Only then,
I am a watcher of the unpreventable.

Master the Construct

Adolescent, or senescent,
the human dispute is set between
inner self-discovery and rationalization.
In its face,
this state of being forming our need of balance
is discontinued.

Inevitably confronted by the construct,
we question logic.
Forced to reach into our hearts and souls,
we are thirsty, famished for answers.

One never obtains the ability to control,
or comprehend its path.
Nowhere written in steps,
and cannot be read from a book,
it is greater than anything.

Within an imprint of a world,
the single aspect shaping our course of life
is this timeless struggle
-the search and pursuit of *love*.

Note to Self

within vigorous competition,
realizing dreams is strictly based on hunger's quantity,
to continue when nearly impossible.

take a chance,
obtain all opportunities in front of you,
for you should demand an undisputed path to the top.

absolute dedication,
it is only an innocent stroke towards distinction from the pack.

reveal your true purpose for commitment,
the desire to aid others,
to build a sophisticated being.

life experiences have enriched you with personal laws:
every moment of every day can be utilized into greatness,
fearlessly fail to succeed,
act with dignified pretermission.

meaningless until proven,
these virtues will be tested for eternity.

so, choose to be involved,
challenge your heart, will,
against the ultimatum of limitations.

Now & Then

Closed mindedness struggles to attain comfort,
unable to accept, change.
Surrounded by complex beliefs, conservatory,
our souls are forced onto a physical and spiritual journey.

Reputation is a decisive motive.
There may be an original poise, gild,
but intimidating personalities constitute significant precipitations.

Even the biological can despise sincerely,
and disown shared blood.
Becoming avoided, and pinned as cursed,
our entire Earthly presence will desire freedom.

A young child's mind is blurred by battling emotions.
As gossip flourishes,
we quickly become the center of attention.
Banned, due to an unexplainable fear,
only following our hearts will light the torch,
and successfully maneuver through the mazes.

Now, the fight for a future plantation is nearly over.
Close the barrier, grow the fruit,
but place the greatest risk on the line.

Bodies fade from the ambitious attempt.
With agony viewed repeatedly,
some will never witness the outcome,
as we eventually experience death.

During the shaky trip,
storms furiously poured,
and maturity was reached.
The trail continues.

Phases

Conflicted personality, estranged mentality...
A piece of realistic purity
within the impossibility of certainty.

Cultures, generations...
A protagonist's meaning by alignment
around separate phases.

Age of innocence, first-half witnesses...
FATHER
MOTHER
Prepare using specific skills.
Execute a frequent ritual.

Adopt this moment of the day,
mixing basic ingredients,
sharing the need for symbolic presence.

Age of awakening, second-half hand...
Similarly masterful, loving
with secret forces of violence,
trembling the innocence.

Cherished memories,
Deep collectivity,
Shattered.

Colliding phases of belonging.
Searches for reconciliation.
Riveting stages throughout the story.

Plain Doubt

Dominion and victimization deployed on many levels.
The isolating discrepancies commemorate an unevenly distributed hierarchy.

Superiority based on attachment,
executing the plan and rules,
a successful solidarity of many under the established reign.

Similar styles and technical approaches,
inserted clues, flashbacks,
representing everyone in the camp.

Some are new, others old,
status differences are shown by duty assignment,
but without clear indications.

Counting the days assures doubt,
depicting some as undeserving of the provided life.

The *plainness* is overpowering.
It weakens, brainwashes.
Trying to teach the mechanics,
a passage of thought calls daughters, dolls.

Many generations pass,
each knowing exactly what is needed,
when they all go about a task.

Portrait

Paused in an impeccable time sequence,
Standing face to face,
I looked deeply straight at her eyes,
Creating a full link between our paths.
In despairing search
And a blink later,
My viewpoint was clear.

Framed in a picture…

Blank thoughts flow steady,
And white walls become my world.
Concentration is set to its limited potential.
My imperative discovery draws a number,
Outlining inconclusive honesty, truth.

Inexistence of people…

Widely stretched windows
Generously offer a panoramic display
Of the glooming night.
With a heavy approach, clueless mind,
I crave to spot shining bright stars,
And numerous constellations.

Invisibility of stars…

Furiously looking across the universe,
My anticipation fades in foretold disappearance.
There are no stars available today,
just endless space.

Possibility of Fear

In the middle of the night,
the thin line between nerves and focus wobbled freely,
as protruding images scraped the hollow walls.

Deforming, shifting,
the spirits were fatal.
Senseless identities, caricatures,
assembled to serve disturbance to my pulse.

I was processed as a victim to
unrestrained violence,
and the seemingly beautiful, undisturbed relaxation.

The intruders danced beneath the doorframe,
waving passed the staircase with pulling white noises.
I was unable to interpret their whispered words,
or the pattern of their purpose.

The floor prevented them from sharing a breath
with the nearly departed life in the squared room.
I sweated unconsciously,
face drowning in depthless frustration.

There were no answers,
or the comfort of protection.
Freedom, courage became foreign realizations.

Closing in on the house's finality.
My door reluctantly cracked in a repeated sequence,
without missing a single tone.

A horrendous light dilated my pupils.
I waited for the image to enter,
and perform its mysterious task.

The unknown maintained the lively fear
in
the
environment.

Roleplaying

A suspenseful circus,
where names are not mentioned.
Beyond the roleplaying, we are scattered sheep,
vestigial, but potentially serviceable.

Homes are obediently arranged,
where our linkages exert order upon possession,
but at the road, we fall down again.

The unawareness of our scruples declines with progression.
Varnished chairs, contradicting ways,
all belong to the eternal web.

The irony is our own reflection.
Each deed escalates by the role in the social network,
and a person's limbic wiring reveals at its deepest layer.

Understanding is staged according to laughter,
as one's search for enjoyment violates the rules.
Regardless if attacked, or if we seek others,
like prey, no other value can be foreseen.

Screening the unevenness,
we could have cleaned the home,
and saved us from ourselves.

Romantic Discovery

The couple sat down on chairs across from each other.
Dancing reflections occupied the room,
with scents of fresh gardens spreading through the wind.

An elusive medium orange mixture of colliding purples, reds,
accumulated into the divine mood of romanticism
deeply hidden behind their silence.

They sat down on a fancy circular table,
scarred with anciently engraved lines,
and symmetrical perfectionisms.
Each individual obscurely glimpsed into the other,
searching for doubting answers.

Skimming around with predetermined purpose,
she arranged elementary objects in playful formations,
he observed her every movement, expression with unlimited patience.

He studied the way she played with her hair on the side of the left ear,
constantly stressing awareness of her flawless appearance.
He noticed the rise of her fragile arm,
as she placed two fingers on her lips,
moving them incautiously by her left cheek, down the neck,
and carelessly back to the original position.

Once he stared down,
she accepted the destined token,
noticing his straight figure,
cleft chin, swimming irises,
a natural proportion in the shoulders,
and the sincere possibility of devoted kindness.
She was evidently surprised.

His manner provoked an innocent smile on her face.
With uprising notions of laughter,
she never realized the immeasurable comfort existing in his company.

Breathing body to body,
their secret was revealing,
as previous nostalgia has subverted.

Savior in a Canvas

The occurrence of light is present,
where all of the delirium exists.
The smudged shadow is shown,
once an outsider becomes apparent.

The analogy arrives by another situation,
an offering of help,
of misery,
becoming a unit during heroic events.

The audience can better imagine distress,
as well as the confrontation between
past harassment with current necessity,
in order to see the course of pain.

The canvas portrays concern,
sensitivity nearly not seen before.
He represents the secure presence of an angel,
willfully risking life for our immortality.

Completely neglecting segregation,
he pulls away from the flames,
grabs her out,
and crawls back in.

In the extinguishment of danger,
equally confused and overwhelmed
by the blame,
a stroke of gratitude gets painted at last.

Setting

It was a usual dark, frigid morning at the lonesome bus stop.
The traffic possessed a drifting motion,
while everyone rushed in dilemma.
The bus arrived, the doors instantly open,
uncertain feelings start racing.

I climbed up the stair, and looked cautiously at the driver.
The operator held a transfer at hand, as if it was a favor.
His face was passionless, omitting all heavenly sensations.

Occupying the front to satisfy the seat-searching contempt,
I imagined the sweaty, contaminated fingerprints,
which tightly held onto each yellow pole.

People of all backgrounds would enter,
wearing stinking, wet apparel.
Most were healthy and some sick,
breathing, touching rhythmically.

The setting was a delusive funeral,
the ultimate job fair,
an opportunity to explore and determine the respected levels of strain.

New entrants were studied, watched carefully.
Once the next exile was identified,
the fight for the empty spot erupted.

The lacking comfort,
drowsiness, and wheeled locomotion,
pressured the passengers into turmoil.

Thoughts of someone speaking were substantial,
but a sharp glance proved the silence's surreal collapse.
When a street name was abruptly announced,
the eyes of many glowed alive.

Victoriously, I was released at last.
The wind's rejuvenation was inhaled once again.
I marched invincibly in triumph,
dreading the upcoming return ride.

Significance of One

Interpretation
Of the morality
Behind
People's
Hearts
During
Times
Of development.
One
Special
Presentation.
Growth
Is dependent
Upon
A child's
Evolvement
To the unacquainted
Everyday
Expectancies.
Due to such
Instability,
A dwelling
Place
Is transformed,
Accompanied by
Comfort
And harmony.
The truth
About one's
Development
Alters
All conventions.
Mixed
Appearances,
Permanent
Exchanges,
Replacing
Acts.
Flawless
Immature
Beliefs.
Realize
Acceptance,
Sustain
Belonging.

Sketch

r *f*
Y e s t e r d a *y*, I sketched the people gap.
ligion *mily*

In connection to the setting,
throughout the ride and my life,
I tried to observe the lamentable truth.

Lying, deception were simply implied
as part of the human condition,
instead of purposeful means.

I developed in a semi-depleted environment,
filled with the imagination of colorful opportunities,
and possessions.

I aim at an elegant appearance constructed for success.
I have wishful thinking for a higher power,
which imparts as the cornerstone in everyone's lives.

bit *je*
T o d a *y*, I sketch the world as a form of deficiency.
erness *lousy*

Understanding modernization's disruption,
as the social enigma.

I am normally an attached person.
Capable of showing great love and hatred equally,
but prefer to laugh through the ticks of spontaneity.

I am a fast-paced individual.
Frequently undergoing nerve-racking exposures,
as it is my most common habit of cracking knuckles
in spiraling patterns.

My eye color is somewhat unidentifiable.
I accept most people,
but hold a precise approach.

prosperi *desi*
T o m o r r o *w*, I will sketch the idea of collectivity.
Y *e*

In determination of prevention,
as a form of aid to human development,
I will attempt to comprehend meaning.

The City by Moonlight

The desolate continuance of flying
implanted in me a desperation
for a physical destination.

Past midnight, I am a magical witness.

In this diminishing night,
the city below sparkles with countless lights,
exposed naked in the face of friendly windows.

The social oblivion is glamorous and the human violence is gentle.

The city seems phantasmagorical,
a place where historic time intervals gather in perfection,
staying motionless among lost emptiness.

A moment of pure fulfilment is near,
while destiny was always the object of Discordia's entertainment.

As the senses lift with epiphany,
the constant of hallucinations master its ritual,
and parallel to the moon's miraculous pull,
identities keep missing the mark.

Looking down, souls explore the possibility of detachment,
and successful spirits become permissible to travel upon forsaken paths.

The city by moonlight is a consecrated sight,
in which I am forced to be a man of discernment,
always leaving a part of myself
within the plane's tracks of hope.

Why

Reality never occurred to me so greatly until recently.
Everything is unusually clear from the hidden blindness,
as if the sun's resurrecting way reached out of its mysterious nature.
Each day fills a part of the gap between the future's hardships,
and a missing allegiance in preparing a soldier.

Being young and repudiated,
modesty would be actual luxury,
but conditions normally brutal are now inspirational.
There always was a significant attachment amongst us,
but we only would exchange mixed words.

In preparation for the masquerade,
I visit him daily, hiding my identity in sorrow.
Despite all efforts, no dream was ever fulfilled,
just living amongst ghosts' mystique,
unaccepted by the rulers of Hell, nor heaven.

I prayed extremely strong,
as if a person was dying in front of me.
At this hour,
the candle's flame had been put away.

My palms are in full contact with the door.
Secondary thoughts pierce through,
like crossed bullets in a destined duel.

I am still unable to escape the repeated whispering,
-"the day has arrived, be proud".

AUTHOR'S NOTE

THANK YOU FOR TAKING THE TIME TO READ THESE SELECTED POEMS WRITTEN OVER THE PERIOD OF 2005-2013. PLEASE TAKE A MOMENT TO LEAVE A COMMENT AND/OR REVIEW.

ABOUT THE AUTHOR

NIKOLAY BOYCHEV was born in 1989, Bulgaria. Educated in Canada and England, he has shown poise in management, consulting, and leadership through his vast international experiences, both professional and philanthropic. He constantly teaches and develops talent, coordinates teams, performs public relations, implements a vast global network among professionals across various fields, and establishes community infrastructure to stay and evolve. With heightened sense of innovation and continuous improvement, he is committed to life-long learning and effectiveness.

*****

APPLIED FREEDOM

selected poems

*****

www.ingramcontent.com/pod-product-compliance
Lightning Source LLC
Chambersburg PA
CBHW021218020426
42331CB00003B/370